Discover Deserts

by Katrina Streza

© 2017 by Katrina Streza
ISBN: 978-1-53240-213-5
eISBN: 978-1-53240-214-2
Images licensed from Fotolia.com
All rights reserved.
No portion of this book may be reproduced
without express permission of the publisher.
First Edition
Published in the United States by
Xist Publishing
www.xistpublishing.com
PO Box 61593 Irvine, CA 92602

A desert is any part of our world that does not get very much rain. Deserts have dry seasons when plants die. This tumbleweed died because it did not get enough water.

3

There are plants that love the desert. This aloe plant keeps water inside and makes a goo that helps with sunburns.

This cactus also keeps water inside. The sharp spines keep animals from the water inside.

7

This cactus flower is bright to let birds and bugs see it from far away. Birds and bugs help the cactus flower grow into a fruit.

This cactus fruit is ready to eat because the spines have been pulled off. The sharp spines keep most animals away.

The desert tortoise loves to eat cactus fruit. They hide from the hot sun and from coyotes but come out to slowly eat grass and other plants.

This is a coyote. When a coyote is hungry, it will eat almost any animal in the desert.

Roadrunners can only fly for a few seconds. They have to run and hide from coyotes and hawks.

17

This jackrabbit has to run quickly to get away from coyotes, bobcats, and mountain lions. His big ears help him listen for danger.

19

This mountain lion, or cougar, hunts in the desert. She will hide behind rocks to wait for an animal to kill.

21

Quail are small birds that live in the desert. They hide under bushes from birds.

This eagle flies high above the desert looking for food. Eagles will eat rabbits or quail.

Small animals in the desert also have to look out for snakes. This gopher snake eats small animals. Gopher snakes cannot hurt people.

Rattlesnakes eat small animals. They can bite people too. They try to scare away other animals by shaking their tails.

Hot deserts are an important part of our world. This lizard would not be happy if it lived anywhere other than the desert.

The desert is hot and dry. Many plants and animals live in the desert.

www.ingramcontent.com/pod-product-compliance
Lightning Source LLC
LaVergne TN
LVHW010020070426
835507LV00001B/22